Getting Organized

A Detailed Guide to Bringing Peacemaking into the Workplace

www.hendrickson.com
www.Peacemaker.net

PEACEMAKER®
MINISTRIES

v 1.1

Table of Contents

Introduction: Why Use THIS Study?

Living Out Your Faith at Work

Do you ever struggle with living out your faith at work? Whether you are a Christian business owner, a leader in your organization, or simply a Christian who spends most of the week working in the marketplace, it's an important question. Have you ever wondered, then, if "success" at work looks different for Christians than it does for non-Christians? As a Christian, you know you are called to live out your beliefs *every* day—not just Sunday mornings, but Thursday afternoons, Monday mornings, and the entire work week.

You are not alone, nor are you the first to face this situation. God has consistently called leaders (Moses, Noah, Daniel, Joseph, Esther, David, and Peter, to name a few) to be faithful to God's principles in the midst of a culture that doesn't accept them. In fact, the culture is often hostile to these principles. Yet as God blessed these men and women in the Bible, he will do likewise with you as you seek to be faithful. God will be with you and guide you as you seek to live out your faith in your organization, home, and community.

> As a Christian, you know you are called to live out your beliefs *every* day—not just Sunday mornings, but Thursday afternoons, Monday mornings, and the entire work week.

The *Resolving Everyday Conflict* study is one practical way to live out your faith wherever you work. Let's think a little more deeply about how it can do that.

Conflict in the Workplace: A Problem You Can't Ignore

It will come as no surprise to you that unresolved conflict at work has significant negative impact. Consider these statistics:

- 53% of workers said they lost time worrying about a confrontation.[1]

- 22% said they put less effort into work because of conflict at the office.[2]

- Employees waste an average of $1,500 and an 8-hour workday for every crucial conversation they avoid (i.e., this is the cost of avoiding a conflict).[3]

Unresolved conflicts often lead to an employee quitting or being dismissed, and that directly impacts the cost of employment:

- Conflicts resulting in the loss of the employee due to quitting or being fired can cost 150% of the employee's annual compensation or as much as 200-250% if the employee is in a managerial position. [4]

Unresolved conflicts also divert appropriate supervision as well as influence key decisions based on broken relationship rather than performance:

- 85% of all workers say they have workplace conflict, yet only 22% of employees say their managers deal well with conflict. [5]
- 60-80% of all difficulties in organizations stem from strained relationships between employees, not from deficits in an individual employee's skill or motivation. [6]

Conflict that happens outside of work also can significantly affect us when we are on the job.

- Employers can lose up to 25% of an employee's productivity due to family strife or divorce. [7]
- On a daily basis, 1 in 5 employees is being negatively affected by a personal issue (e.g., addiction, grief, divorce, care-giving, stress, depression). [8]
- 49% of employees lose an hour of productivity or more each day due to stress. [9]
- Almost half of employees cite stress and personal issues as the most common reason for work absence. [10]

You've likely seen all these negative effects of conflict played out in the lives and careers of those who work at your organization. And it's great that you want to do something about it (otherwise you wouldn't be interested in the *Resolving Everyday Conflict* study, right?). As a leader, you want to equip your team members with life skills that will not only make the workplace more productive, but also help them outside of the workplace. And that's just what *Resolving Everyday Conflict* does.

Resolving Conflict Biblically

Much has already been written about applying biblical principles in the workplace.[11] On the other hand, little has been written about how conflicts are opportunities to model and live out our faith in the workplace, as well as to serve others and give glory to God.

There are lots of tools and techniques out there that seek to change the behaviors that contribute to conflict. These tools usually focus on "managing" the conflict by eliminating it or at least by avoiding aspects of it, believing that this will enhance our work and make us more productive. This might *seem* like a good way to handle the problem. It might also seem like the quickest way to deal with conflict.

But it doesn't get to the underlying cause. Therefore, it won't lead to real transformation. Once you get to the *cause*, then and only then can you make lasting changes that not only restore relationships, but also equip people to address *future* conflicts productively.

The *Resolving Everyday Conflict* study (including the steps outlined in this booklet) gets to those underlying causes, providing you with the tools to introduce your staff to principles that will help them transform how they address conflicts. This is a unique opportunity for you to invest in your staff—equipping them with valuable life skills that impact them *both at home and at work*.

As you go through this study, you will be able to model your faith in your work and through the relationships within your organization. And that's an exciting way to connect the faith you profess on Sunday morning to the way you live the rest of your week.

What's in this booklet?

The rest of this booklet answers the following questions:

- **Running the Study**

  - Who is this study for?

  - How does the study work?

  - How do I get started?

  - Who should lead the study?

  - What if it becomes personal?

- **After the Study**

  - What other steps do I need to take to make biblical conflict resolution a part of the culture of our organization?

> "In today's society, it [resolving conflict according to biblical principles] is revolutionary because people in my profession generally think the first thing you need to do is go to the courthouse."
>
> *Peter Dobelbower, General Counsel*
> *Hobby Lobby*

Running the Study

Who is the study for?

The short answer is simple: Everyone at your organization!

An organization with a common understanding of how to address conflict biblically will be able to better handle those conflicts that naturally occur at work. This organization will also be prepared to help one another, leading to a more productive and satisfying work environment for everyone. But let's get a little more specific:

> An organization with a common understanding of how to address conflict biblically will be able to better handle those conflicts that naturally occur at work.

- **Every staff member** will benefit from learning and understanding biblical principles for resolving conflict at work and at home.

- **Managers and supervisors** (including human relations staff) will benefit from understanding these basic principles and putting them into practice. They'll also start to be equipped to help staff members to address the daily conflicts that frequently distract them from their work.

- **Leaders of the organization** will benefit from the study as they learn the same principles that they desire their staff to apply. As the leaders learn and apply these principles to their own lives, they are then able to model these principles in their relationships and interactions with staff and others working with the organization.

Is the study appropriate for non-Christians?

Although the principles in *Resolving Everyday Conflict* are taken from the Bible, many of them represent commonly accepted values of our Western culture. You don't necessarily have to be a Christian to understand and apply these principles. Principles like honesty, integrity, trust, respectful communication, and gentleness are all principles people value and would agree are important to their relationships.

BIBLICAL ANSWERS FOR A COMMON PROBLEM

Nevertheless, the content of the study is still clearly based on principles taken from the Bible and makes reference to biblical passages, stories, and concepts—*it is an **explicitly** biblical study*. Generally, we'd say that this study is intended for Christians, although non-Christians can definitely still find value in it.

Offering the study: voluntary or mandatory?

Can you offer this study, then, even if you employ individuals without regard to their religious beliefs? And can you invite people who do not share the Christian faith to this study?

The answer to both questions is yes, particularly if you make the study voluntary.

As a general rule, employers can offer training programs that are based on principles taken from the Bible, but cannot require staff to undergo religious training, participate in religious services, or engage in behavior that would violate their sincerely held religious beliefs.[12] In addition, be careful not to give the employee the impression that they have to agree with the employer's religious beliefs in order to keep his or her job or get a promotion.[13] You will also want to consult your attorney for guidance if you believe this may be a question for some of your staff.[14]

How does the study work?

This study contains eight 30-minute lessons on DVD. You should allow at least an hour for each session (you'll need an hour to watch the DVD and then to discuss questions in the study guide). The study is pretty flexible—you could schedule the study over eight consecutive weeks, over four weeks (allowing two hours per session), or even use as a one-and-a-half-day training.

> "Our group was so excited to learn all of the principles and put them into practice that we decided to meet over eight successive workdays (during our lunch hour)."
>
> *Dianna Bradley, Chaplain*
> *Hobby Lobby*

As you plan, you will want to think about these things:

- Choose meeting times that are convenient for your staff. (For instance, a brown bag lunch might work well.)

- Select a comfortable location for everyone, with plenty of places to sit (e.g., a conference room, a lunch room, or other space with appropriate privacy).

- Have a television and DVD player that can be easily operated and easily seen.

- Allow enough time.

  - Again, remember that each video contains about 30 minutes of teaching, followed by at least 20 to 30 minutes of discussion and prayer. (If you have more time available, you can easily spend more time on discussion.) Group leaders should allow at least 60 minutes, plus time for informal conversation as the group assembles.

  - Be sure that your group leaders know to begin on time and to close the session at the pre-arranged time.

  - Remind your group leaders to **read their Leader's Guide**. It will prepare them for the session and give them confidence to help others apply the principles in the study. The Leader's Guide contains guidance on:

    - How to lead well as the group discusses the material

    - Key insights to the material

    - Additional discussion questions

    - References to additional reading

> **Preparation is key!**
>
> Remind your group leaders to prepare ahead of time by:
>
> - Watching the video
>
> - Reading the Group Leader's Guide
>
> - Praying through the content of the week's session.

How do we get started?

Engage Your Leaders First

You may want to have the leadership (managers, supervisors, etc.) go through the study before offering it to the whole organization. This will lay a great foundation because leaders will have an understanding of the principles that are taught, will be able to model them, and also can help other staff members to incorporate them into the workplace.

Show the invitation video at your next leadership meeting (this video is found on DVD 4 of the

DVD set and is also available at www.Peacemaker.net/REC-invite). Begin talking about the conflicts in your organization as a leadership team and how you currently address them. Talk about what works and what doesn't work.

Invite your staff

Here are some helpful guidelines for encouraging your staff to attend the study:

- Four to six weeks prior to offering the study, use the REC invitation video during appropriate staff meetings or in other staff communication. You'll need to show the video and verbally promote the study *more than once* to make sure that everybody hears about it.

> **For other promotional materials go to:**
>
> www.Peacemaker.net/REC-promo

- Communicate two themes:

  - **Everybody** struggles with conflict—people of every age and stage, and both at work and at home.

  - **Everybody** can benefit from this practical biblical study—even people who do not necessarily accept the Christian faith or who have no commitment to a church can learn from these principles, which provide real and practical solutions to the conflicts of daily life.

- Place the invitation video (www.Peacemaker.net/REC-invite) on your company or employee website and consistently remind people about it. Highlight portions of the video teaching during appropriate meetings and times. This will give people a good taste of the practical teaching that's included in the study.

Who should lead the study?

Any individual who has leadership abilities and is comfortable facilitating a small group discussion can effectively lead the study. A detailed Leader's Guide is provided along with other background materials to help the leader prepare well for each session. (NOTE: The leader will need to do some preparation in advance of each session to be ready to facilitate.)

It may be appropriate and beneficial to have leaders within your organization be the designated leaders of the study.

What if it becomes personal?

Conflict is often an uncomfortable part of our lives. This study doesn't shy away from addressing this reality, even if it gets uncomfortable. As it encourages people to deal honestly with their conflicts, the study may cause people to "get personal"—identifying issues in their own lives that need to be addressed. Some conflicts that come up may involve situations at home or in facets of their personal lives outside of work. That is actually a good thing—it means that people are genuinely facing their struggles and seeking help when they need it.

> As it encourages people to deal honestly with their conflicts, the study may cause people to "get personal"—identifying issues in their own lives that need to be addressed.

But it also means that your group leader will want to be prepared for these situations by having a plan on how to assist group members who are facing conflict. The group leader may personally assist that individual, be prepared to pass along resources, or refer the individual to someone else in the organization for assistance. As you make this plan, follow these guidelines:

- Remind participants that information shared with one another is confidential within the group. (Ask group members to agree to this commitment at the beginning of the study.) This assurance of confidentiality will allow people to be appropriately transparent.

- Be considerate of one another, speaking only that which is helpful to building others up according to their needs. A gracious and encouraging word by the group leader can make all the difference in helping someone to respond well.

- Be prepared to address workplace conflicts in a manner consistent with your organization's policies and consistent with the principles taught in the study. *We recommend that the people in your organization who are responsible for addressing workplace conflict complete the study before offering it to the entire organization.*

- Give an overview of your organization's conflict resolution or grievance policy. (If you don't have such a policy, we've included a sample later in this booklet.) Current conflicts taking place at work are likely to come out during the study, and you will want to make sure participants know what they are supposed to do.

- Depending upon the size of your organization, get the legal, HR, and training departments involved up front so they can provide support after the study. Individuals in those departments may desire to take more specific training in the area of Conflict Coaching (see the information on **Additional Training** on page 15).

- If you have an organizational chaplain, referring those in conflict to the chaplain is often an appropriate response. You may also want to have a list of churches that have Peacemaking Teams or staff trained in peacemaking and/or counseling that would be willing to receive referrals.

After the Study

Embedding These Principles in the Culture of Your Organization

Offering a *Resolving Everyday Conflict* study at your workplace is a foundational step to take to help your organization begin to deal with conflict in a more biblical manner. But it's by no means the only step. Like any study, information that is simply transmitted and not applied will not last. And we know you want these principles to last. This section discusses four other key steps that you should consider as you think about how to embed biblical peacemaking principles long-term into the culture of your organization:

1. **Update your organization's policies** to reflect the principles of biblical conflict resolution.

2. **Implement a biblical conflict resolution process** for employment disputes.

3. **Use conciliation clauses** in your agreements with third parties.

4. **Offer additional training** to select employees on biblical peacemaking.

1. Update your organization's policies to reflect the principles of biblical conflict resolution.

The first area to consider is to **make changes to your current policies** so that they explicitly include guidance on how conflicts between individuals are to be resolved. Your organization's employment manual and other policies should note where employees can receive help as they follow the conflict resolution process. Sample employment policies can be found in Appendix A, beginning on page 19. Please read through the sample policies and consider the changes you might make to your own policies. Be particularly conscious of addressing the following points in your policy:

- Encourage one-to-one resolution of conflicts.

- Give guidance on the basic principles for resolving conflict, and point staff to conflict resolution training and resources (e.g., the *Resolving Everyday Conflict* study).

- Provide a process for your staff to seek help in going one-to-one.

- Provide a process for your staff to get help resolving conflicts if their one-to-one efforts are not successful.

- Explain how to request help and how that help will be implemented.

- Address how to get help if the conflict is between people of different authority levels (e.g., a supervisor and a member of his staff).

- Provide an alternative dispute resolution process (other than a lawsuit) that is based on biblical principles (see Section 2 below).

One organization that made this sort of change to their policies gave this testimony of the impact those policies had:

Our company recently revised its discipline and grievance policy to include principles of biblical peacemaking. We have already used these principles to resolve four employee conflicts, with significant relational and economic benefits. In one case, gossip and back-stabbing seriously damaged the relationships of four of our key employees. As the human resources director, I spent six hours coaching and mediating, which resulted in sincere confession and forgiveness. In addition to retaining valuable staff, we saved at least $15,000 in recruiting, relocation, and training costs. Our CEO was delighted that we had recouped the entire cost of my training [with Peacemaker Ministries] seven-fold by resolving just one dispute!

In another case, we found it necessary to dismiss the employee, but having undergirded our process with these principles, we were thoroughly prepared when, a few weeks after the employee was dismissed, we received an Equal Employment Opportunity Commission (EEOC) claim. Because we had handled this matter with the dignity and honesty that Peacemaker Ministries teaches, we felt confident that we had a strong case. The case was dismissed by the EEOC, resulting in only nominal attorney fees. By investing just six hours in peacemaking, we avoided a prolonged and expensive legal process.

When we discovered that one of our workers was involved in unethical behavior, our first thought was simply to fire her. But we remembered the "three opportunities of conflict" and decided to make a serious effort to help her. Instead of becoming angry and threatening us with a retaliatory lawsuit, she resigned voluntarily. Best of all, she committed herself to a counseling program we recommended. In a recent letter she wrote, "I am so glad that my problem was exposed while I was working for you. God has used you to turn my life around."

Liz Sherrell, Operations Director
King's Ranch and Hannah Homes, Alabama

2. Implement a biblical conflict resolution process for employment disputes.

Another step you will want to consider is including a process for **biblically-based alternative dispute resolution** in your employment agreements.

Civil litigation is perhaps the *worst* way to resolve employment disputes. You may very well have seen that first-hand. As a result, many companies have adopted an alternative dispute resolution system involving *secular* mediation and arbitration. As beneficial as such processes can be, they are not capable of achieving the self-examination and deep reconciliation that can result from *biblically* guided mediation and arbitration.

> Civil litigation is perhaps the *worst* way to resolve employment disputes.

Although companies may not be able to require employees to participate in a biblical process, they can provide a dual-track system that gives employees the option of choosing either a secular or a biblical process to address employment-related legal disputes. A detailed process and diagram of the Dual-Track Process and sample language for an employment conflict resolution process is included in Appendix B.

*"I held private doubts that our mediation was an exercise, a prelude to the arbitration where **real** resolution could be enforced. I was wrong. The mediation was all that was necessary for the parties to be heard and for the healing to take place, to the glory of God!"*

— A party in a contract dispute

3. Use conciliation clauses in your agreements with third parties.

Another way to provide a positive Christian witness and avoid expensive litigation is to **include conciliation clauses** in contracts with outside clients and vendors. These legally enforceable clauses require that if a dispute cannot be resolved through personal negotiation, it must be resolved through biblical mediation or arbitration (rather than litigation). Here again, a commitment to following biblical principles can produce many benefits as described by this attorney:

> *"My client had a major breach of contract claim against another company. The contract included a conciliation clause, but since I thought we would do better in civil court, I advised my client to seek a court order voiding the clause. The judge held the clause to be enforceable, however, so we were forced to submit the case to a conciliator appointed by Peacemaker Ministries. I was not enthused about the process and approached it in an adversarial way. But soon I got pulled into the conciliatory spirit of the process. Within a few hours both parties recognized their personal responsibility for the problem and arrived at a mutually satisfactory agreement. Even though I had fought to avoid Christian conciliation, I was so impressed with the outcome that I am now training to be a conciliator myself."*

> — An attorney representing a party in a mediation

Sample language that has been used in countless contracts and has been consistently enforced by both state and federal courts can be found in Appendix C, along with helpful facts concerning these clauses and their use. You can also find sample clauses online at www.iccpeace.com/GuidelinesHandout/index.html under "Conciliation Clauses."

4. Offer additional training to select employees on biblical peacemaking.

Many managers and human relations staff have never received adequate training on resolving conflict. They are usually told that they *should* make peace, but they are seldom taught *how* to do it in practical terms. Many Christian-led businesses are making up for this deficit by giving their managers and HR staff the option of receiving training through Peacemaker Ministries.

> Staff members are usually told that they *should* make peace, but they are seldom taught *how* to do it in practical terms.

The *Resolving Everyday Conflict* study is just the beginning of getting equipped to be a peacemaker. Many more **training opportunities** are available that will further equip your staff to be a helpful resource in conflict situations. Specifically:

- **Provide further training using an *implicitly* biblical methodology** – Peacemaker Ministries offers custom training on "Transforming Conflict in the Workplace," where your managers and leaders will apply the principles of peacemaking (taught without use of Scripture or biblical language so that both Christians and non-Christians can take part) in their daily work, helping them to effectively model the principles themselves. This training also will equip your designated group of leaders to guide and help others resolve conflicts with other staff members on an informal and internal basis. Contact Peacemaker Ministries at 800-711-7118 for information regarding this training.

- **Provide training using an *explicitly* biblical methodology** – Peacemaker Ministries also provides an extensive, biblical, live training in *conflict coaching* (counseling one person on how to resolve a conflict) and *mediation* (facilitating reconciliation between two or more people), following the *Rules of Procedure for Christian Conciliation*. You can learn more about this training at www.iccpeace.com/Training or contact Peacemaker Ministries at 800-711-7118 to discuss how this training can be provided to your organization.

A Final Word of Encouragement

Developing and implementing a biblical peacemaking system in an organization requires a deliberate investment of time and training. The long-term dividends of this investment far outweigh the costs. The benefits include not only saving valuable time, staff, and money, but also—and more importantly—giving a practical witness to the wisdom of God's Word and the reconciling power of Jesus Christ. We are delighted that you are taking the initiative to make this investment, and we will be praying for you as you go through this process. May God bless you and your organization as you seek to live out your faith where you work.

Appendices

Appendix A: Sample Employment Policies

NOTE: The following samples are provided for information purposes only, and do not constitute legal advice. You should consult your attorney regarding the use of these provisions and the application of any specific State or Federal law to their use and enforceability.

Conflict Resolution Policy

SAMPLE #1

It is the intent and hope of the Company that disputes and conflicts between employees and/or related to employment be addressed in a manner which is consistent with the values of the Company. Accordingly, an employee who is a party to a conflict or dispute with another employee is encouraged to address the conflict directly with the other person involved in the conflict in an effort to resolve it. In the event that this effort is unsuccessful, the employee should seek the assistance and involvement of his or her immediate supervisor who may be able to facilitate the resolution of the conflict by applying principles outlined within this policy.

An attempt to resolve the conflict under the Conflict Resolution Policy does not prevent an employee from utilizing the Open Door Policy.

The Four Principles for Peacemaking

Employees should approach conflict resolution in a manner that does more than simply resolves disputes, but also serves others, helps the involved people grow, provides an example of the Company's values, and leads to a more productive and cooperative working relationship between employees. Employees should consider the following peacemaking principles when attempting to resolve conflict:

1. *Go to Higher Ground:* Employees should see conflict as the opportunity to clarify and live out their highest values and beliefs. Employees should evaluate each conflict to see whether there is an opportunity for forgiveness.

2. *Get Real About Yourself:* Employees should take responsibility for their contributions to conflicts before criticizing others.

3. *Gently Engage Others:* An employee in conflict should affirm the relationship with the person with whom he or she is in conflict and confront that person respectfully.

4. *Get Together in Lasting Solutions:* Employees can preserve relationships through genuine reconciliation and fair solutions.

If an employee is interested in applying the above principles to a conflict, he or she should contact his or her supervisor, the Chaplain's Office, or the Human Resources Department for guidance.

This policy is used by permission from Hobby Lobby's Employee Handbook.

SAMPLE #2

Introduction

Normal Application of Principles Regarding Dealing with Conflict Biblically

The following steps are Organization's administrative procedures for dealing with grievances and conflict. They are also the steps members and employees are encouraged to apply personally in dealing with conflicts and grievances. Generally, the steps would be followed in order, but there are options along the way.

The goal is to keep the resolution of any grievance as informal as possible and at the lowest level possible, to seek wise and godly counsel from people close to the situation who understand the surrounding circumstances, and to involve as few people in the process as possible.

Personal Preparation for Dealing with Conflicts

When conflicts arise it is wise to have a time of personal preparation. The parties involved should endeavor to adopt a godly attitude, considering their own responsibility in the matter and committing to confronting gently and constructively.

It should be recognized that often, in dealing with conflicts in a biblical manner, the offended parties can, and perhaps should, given the circumstances, overlook the wrong done to them. Overlooking an offense is appropriate when the offended party is able to forgive the offender and move ahead without suppressed feelings of bitterness or anger. At any stage in the process of working through a conflict, an offended party may choose to forgive the other party and not pursue the issue any farther.

Please remember that the following are principles and there is freedom to vary from them if indicated by a specific situation. The facts of the situation should be carefully considered, including the culture of those involved.

In many of these steps the Administration does not need or want to be formally involved. Where a third party's help is necessary, where there is a conflict or grievance involving different levels of authority, or where there is a claim or allegation that the employee or organization has failed to comply with provisions in a conflict, the matter will be addressed, by agreement, according to the Organization's dispute resolution process. [NOTE: Language describing this process is found on page 30.]

STEP 1: Starting to Deal with Conflict

An employee who has a conflict with another employee should consider the following options for dealing with the issues of their particular conflict. The following activities are not a required sequence. Parties are free to select or combine them, omitting any which seem likely to be ineffective or counterproductive as indicated by the situation.

> **'One-on-One':** Considering the principles found in Matthew 18:15-17, one party can go to the other party to make their feelings and concerns known.
>
> AND/OR ...

Seek the Help of a Friend/Coach: In dealing with the issues of a conflict it is often a good idea to seek the help of a friend or someone who can perform the role of a "coach." This friend or coach can help a person prepare to raise the issues that need to be addressed. Friend/coach is used here as someone who advises one of the parties in a conflict on how to work through a problem. It should be noted that this coaching is done without the presence of the other party. It is intended to assist the person being coached to approach the other party in the way that will be most likely to bring resolution.

Possible Outcomes

Resolution

It is hoped that resolution can be achieved at this stage between the individuals involved and that no further steps will be necessary. Resolution may take (three) different forms.

Restoration: Open, healthy relationship between the parties.

Constructive Separation: Sometimes constructive separation is a positive step. Parties may not see eye to eye, but they agree to disagree respectfully. An acknowledgement that two individuals are not able to work together may be considered a satisfactory resolution, and should not be taken as an indication of failure.

Continue to options under Dispute Resolution (Mediation). [See page 30.]

This policy is used by permission from "SIL-PNG's" Employee Handbook.

Appendix B: Sample Employment Dispute Resolution Process

Including a biblically-based process for the resolution of conflict will ensure that the biblical principles are applied in even the more difficult conflicts you may face. Most employment contracts include "alternative dispute resolution" clauses, where the employer and the employee agree that any dispute arising out of the employment relationship will be resolved under a process which does NOT include the courts. (Sample contract language is found in Appendix C as well as at the end of this section.) It starts with mediation, followed by legally binding arbitration if the mediation does not result in a resolution.

The following is a dual-track dispute resolution process which allows the employee, while agreeing to use an alternative dispute resolution process, to elect at the time of the conflict between a biblically-based process or a secular-based process. The following is a diagram and explanation of the process and how the election is made.

Dual-Track Conflict Resolution Process

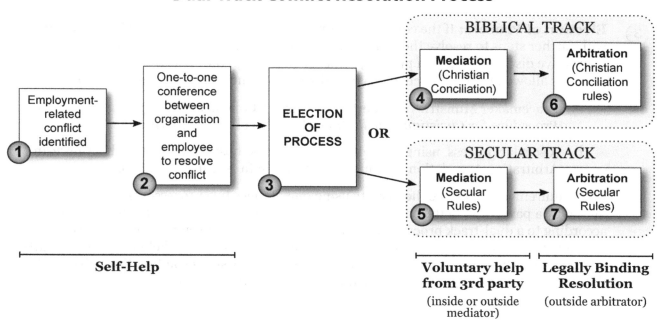

This dual-track system has seven possible steps:

① **Conflict Identified:** It begins when the organization and employee recognize that there is an employment-related conflict that has not been resolved by applying the Conflict Resolution policies and process in the Employee Handbook for addressing conflicts. (See section on employment policies in Appendix A.)

Peer conflicts are usually addressed under the Conflict Resolution Policy, unless it rises to a discipline or performance issue. Discipline and performance issues are usually addressed according to the organization's performance guidelines. If these do not resolve the conflict and the matter is one which is believed to be a claim of a failure to abide by the employment agreement or relationship, it is appropriate for the organization and the employee to move to Step 2.

② **One-to-one Meeting:** Step 2 directs the organizational representative and the employee to attempt to resolve the conflict on a one-to-one basis applying biblical principles as set forth in the Conflict Resolution Policy discussed in Appendix A.

③ **Election of Process:** If the conflict is not resolved, and the employee desires to proceed with further steps to resolve the dispute, the employee is required to do so pursuant to an alternative dispute resolution process, rather than through the civil court system. The employee is allowed to elect which alternative dispute resolution process they wish to use:

    a. Peacemaker Ministries or a Certified Christian Conciliator™, applying the *Rules of Procedure for Christian Conciliation* [15] (a "biblical" process); **or**

    b. A secular process, using rules of process such as those developed by the American Arbitration Association or similar organization (a "secular" process).

This requirement to resolve the dispute using one of these two processes is usually required by a paragraph in the employment contract. (Sample language requiring resolution according to a dual-track process can be found on page 26.) The agreement can also be entered at the time the conflict is identified and it is recognized that help from a third party is needed. It is best, however, if those involved agree to pursue resolution through one of these two processes as part of creating the employment relationship.

(4) **Biblical Mediation:** If a biblical process is chosen, the organization and employee can choose to have the matter addressed with the help of a third person acting as a mediator. Mediation is a voluntary process whereby the organization and the employee, with the help of a third person, seek to reach a resolution of the dispute by mutual agreement. This process can be provided through one of two alternative mediation opportunities:

1. A **formal mediation**, using a mediator selected from outside the organization applying the Rules of Procedure for Christian Conciliation (www.iccpeace.com /Rules). The mediator is selected through Peacemaker Ministries administering the process, or by mutual agreement to use a Certified Christian Conciliator. More information on this process can be found at www.iccpeace.com/Guidelines.

2. An **informal mediation** using a mediator from within the organization, trained in Christian Conciliation, applying the *Rules of Procedure for Christian Conciliation*. When managers and HR staff are well trained, they will usually be able to resolve a dispute short of arbitration.

(5) If a secular process is chosen, the choice is similar to Step 4 above, with the exception that the process is based on a set of secular rules such as those provided by the American Arbitration Association. This process can be provided through one of two alternative mediation opportunities:

1. A **formal mediation**, using a mediator selected from outside the organization applying American Arbitration Association or similar rules and a mediator from the American Arbitration Association or similar secular organization.

2. An **informal mediation** using a mediator from within the organization applying secular rules of procedure.

(6) If the employee and organization are unable to reach a mutual resolution, the dispute moves to arbitration. Arbitration is a process in which the people involved agree to have a third party decide the substantive issue in dispute, with the decision being legally binding on the employee and the organization. The arbitration is conducted according to the *Rules of Procedure for Christian Conciliation*, using an arbitrator(s) appointed by Peacemaker Ministries. The arbitrator(s) is a Certified Christian Conciliator.

If the employee and organization are unable to reach a mutual resolution, and elect to use a secular process for resolving the dispute, the dispute moves to arbitration, using American Arbitration Association or similar rules of procedure and an arbitrator(s) selected by the employee and organization.

This dual-track process can be included in standard employment conflict resolution language in employment contracts. The following is a sample conciliation clause, providing a dual track process, which can be included in an employment contract:[16]

> The parties to this employment agreement mutually agree to submit all employment-related legal disputes (excluding claims for benefits under workers' compensation, unemployment compensation laws, and ERISA-governed benefit plans) between any employee and the Company to mediation, and if such mediation is unsuccessful, to binding arbitration. Mediation and if necessary, binding arbitration shall be in lieu of the right to file a lawsuit in Court or other administrative agency. The parties intend that this agreement waives the right to resolve any such dispute by filing a lawsuit.

> The mediation and arbitration shall be conducted either under a process according to the Rules of Procedure for Christian Conciliation, administered by the Institute for Christian Conciliation, which applies biblical principles in the mediation and arbitration proceedings (copies of the Rules and information regarding this process can be reviewed at www.iccpeace.com), or according to American Arbitration Association's National Rules for the Resolution of Employment Disputes (the Rules can be reviewed at www. adr.org), at the election of the employee.

> At the time the employee or company submits the dispute to mediation and/or arbitration, the employee will be asked to select which process or Rules and mediation/arbitration provider organization to mediate and/or arbitrate the matter. A more detailed explanation of this election process is attached to the contract. [It is suggested that the diagram and explanation of the Dual Track Process above be attached to the employment contract.]

Dispute Resolution Process Explanation for Employee Handbooks

NOTE: The following samples are provided for information purposes only, and do not constitute legal advice. You should consult your attorney regarding the use of these provisions and the application of any specific State or Federal law to their use and enforceability.

The Dual Track Process should also be included and explained in an employee handbook. The following are samples of how this process can be incorporated into an employment handbook.

SAMPLE #1

Submission of Disputes to Binding Arbitration

All employees and the Company mutually agree to submit all employment-related legal disputes (excluding claims for benefits under workers' compensation, unemployment compensation laws, and ERISA-governed benefit plans) between any employee and the Company to binding arbitration. All Company employees are required to sign and return a Mutual Arbitration Agreement as a condition of their employment and continued employment. The Mutual Arbitration Agreement is included at the end of this Employee Handbook.

Arbitration is mutually beneficial to both the Company and its employees. Arbitration provides:

1. *Speed.* Court proceedings are cumbersome, complicated, and lengthy. The arbitration process is less complicated and quicker.

2. *Reduced cost.* Employees and the Company will save money by avoiding the costly expense of court litigation. The arbitrator's fee and administrative costs assessed by the arbitrator and/or arbitration provider will be borne solely by the Company.

3. *Experienced decision maker.* The arbitration procedures require an arbitrator to be experienced in employment-related disputes. For more than thirty years, the United States Supreme Court has encouraged employees and employers to take

advantage of arbitrators' experience and knowledge.

Arbitration under the Mutual Arbitration Agreement between employees and the Company shall be conducted by either the Employment Arbitration Rules and Mediation Procedures or the Institute for Christian Conciliation and pursuant to the American Arbitration Association's National Rules for the Resolution of Employment Disputes or the Institute for Christian Conciliation's Rules of Procedure for Christian Conciliation, respectively, and any other applicable rules then in effect. At the time the employee submits the dispute to arbitration, the employee will be asked to select which arbitration provider organization to arbitrate the matter: either the Employment Arbitration Rules and Mediation Procedures or the Institute for Christian Conciliation.

Every effort has been made to ensure that all employees have access to a copy of the applicable arbitration rules and procedures as adopted by the Employment Arbitration Rules and Mediation Procedures and those adopted by the Institute for Christian Conciliation. Employees may review the arbitration rules and procedures by:

1. Requesting a copy or copies from the employee's supervisor;

2. Requesting a copy or copies from the Company's Human Resources Department at (555) 123-4567; or

3. Reviewing the complete set of up-to-date rules, forms, procedures and guides available from the Employment Arbitration Rules and Mediation Procedures and the Institute for Christian Conciliation by viewing their websites at www.adr.org and www.peacemaker.net, respectively.

Please review these rules and procedures carefully.

This policy is used by permission from Hobby Lobby's Employee Handbook.

If a conflict is not resolved through "one-on-one" efforts (see STEP 1: Starting to Deal with Conflict on page 21), a third party should assist. Third party assistance is appropriate where the conflict involves differing levels of authority or if mediation/arbitration is desired.

Conflict/Grievance Involving Differing Levels of Authority

It is the desire of Employer that a member or employee with a conflict or grievance involving a person in authority be able to get the help of a third party when desired. This third party shall assist in securing the attention of the person in authority and in presenting a respectful request for reconsideration, or in pointing out how a decision or situation is believed to have been mishandled.

Mediation may be appropriate while it is still possible for a decision to be changed. Grievance conciliation, when an unwelcome decision is already in effect, will primarily focus on personal understanding and reconciliation, both of which are highly valued.

Staff members trained as mediators, in addition to helping those under authority in these situations, will also do their best to encourage the person in authority to come to the discussion with an appropriate attitude. It is the desire of Organization to establish an ethos that expects and encourages concerned members to use this process. It is recognized as providing help to both the aggrieved member or employee and the person in authority.

Following are some considerations particular to those in authority and to those under authority. There are some distinctions in the application of these procedures to conflicts involving differing levels of authority, particularly in the application of Steps 1 and 2 below.

For those in authority:

Those in authority should keep themselves open to being approached by those with a grievance or a request for reconsideration, or someone representing such parties. They should maintain and communicate an attitude of willingness to admit and learn from mistakes. It is vital that those in authority be willing to listen to respectful requests for reconsideration of their decisions, and also to suggestions about perceived failures in how matters have been handled. Those in authority are also able to turn to a coach for advice and help if they have a disagreement with someone under their authority, or they need protection from an attack on them. Those in authority should also remember the steps of personal preparation mentioned above when bringing problems to the attention of those they supervise.

For those under authority:

Those under authority should present grievances or requests for reconsideration with respect for the position of authority. They should remember that reconsideration of a decision will only be possible with the consent of the individual who made the decision. It is important to maintain and communicate a commitment to submit to those in authority. Those aggrieved are encouraged to seek informal coaching help before approaching a person in authority, as to do otherwise can easily be counter-productive. Adequate pre-mediation coaching is especially important.

When "one-on-one" efforts (see Step 1 on page 21) are not successful, the parties involved are to seek assistance through a third party, starting with Step 2 below.

STEP 2: Mediation

The parties experiencing conflict may seek Mediation, either informal (2A), or formal (2B). This mediation is intended to try to help the parties hear each other and work out their grievance or conflict. In some cases, Step 2 may be the initial step towards conflict resolution.

The Branch Administration maintains a roster of individuals who have been selected and have agreed to serve on an "on call" basis to help resolve grievances.

The Steps in the Mediation Process given below are those that will be followed in formal mediation and may be helpful in informal mediation, as well.

STEP 2A - Informal Mediation

This ranges from a mutually acceptable friend helping two parties to talk together, to something much more intentional, with two trained mediators leading mediation according to its basic principles, but without any of the formality. No records are kept, and nothing is reported to anyone at the end. A written decision is still possible but only if the issue needs an agreement that both parties want on paper. Mediators are always expected to maintain confidentiality.

STEP 2B - Formal Mediation

Formal Mediation may be either voluntary or imposed by the appropriate supervisor of the members involved, whether a manager, division administrator, or member of the directorate.

Voluntary:

No records are kept, and nothing is reported to anyone at the end, except as agreed by the parties involved. A written decision is encouraged but not required.

Parties requesting formal mediation should ask for the names of the trained mediators. However, if both parties do not agree to pursue mediation, one party may submit a written request to their supervisor for intervention. The request should include the following:

i)   names and contact information for all parties involved;

ii) a brief statement of the circumstances of the situation, including dates;

iii) a brief recounting of the steps already taken to resolve the situation;

iv) a statement of the resolution desired.

In the case of a request for mediation by one party, the supervisor receiving the request will notify the other party concerned of the request for formal intervention. If the other party is still unwilling to enter mediation, the supervisor shall decide whether or not to impose mediation.

Imposed:

The situations in which a person in authority might find it appropriate to impose mediation include known unresolved interpersonal conflict, broken relationships that are affecting people's ability to work together, etc.

The supervisor initiating the mediation will receive a written report. This will include the results of the mediation, but not necessarily the details of the conflict or grievance.

Formation of Formal Mediation Team

Each party in the dispute will choose one individual to serve on the Formal Mediation Team from the list of mediators. The mediators must be acceptable to both parties, and must be willing to serve together. However, if the parties are unable to agree, mediators will be assigned.

Note: At any level in the process, if an individual's relationship is too close to those involved in the grievance to remain adequately impartial in their role as a mediator, the individual should excuse himself or herself and another person should be appointed to mediate.

At the earliest opportunity the Formal Mediation Team should meet together with the parties and begin the process described below.

Steps in the Mediation Process

   a. The mediators are given any pertinent background information available prior to meeting with the parties involved. This is confidential information that will be handled discreetly.

   b. This process will normally be preceded by separate pre-mediation sessions with each of the parties involved, possibly including the process of shuttle diplomacy outlined under Intermediation above.

c. Setting expectations: Mediators will outline the process and review ground rules.

d. Understanding what and why: All parties will be asked to tell their story and to express their feelings.

e. Clarifying and wording issues: Identifying each issue that needs to be addressed and seeking a neutral way to express it.

f. Exploring interests and solutions: Identifying each party's interests regarding each issue and seeking solutions that will bring those interests together.

g. Solidifying agreement and plans: Finalizing solutions and commitments. It is good to put the agreement in writing.

Possible Outcomes

Resolution

It is the expectation of (Organization) that conflicts and grievances that have not been resolved in the early stages (Step 1) will be resolved in through Mediation (Step 2). As in Step 1, resolution may take three different forms.

Restoration: Open, healthy relationship between the parties.

Constructive Separation: Sometimes constructive separation is a positive step. Parties may not see eye to eye, but they agree to disagree respectfully. An acknowledgement that two individuals are not able to work together may be considered a satisfactory resolution, and should not be taken as an indication of failure.

Continue to options under STEP 3

Arbitration: If there are still unresolved issues regarding tangible matters, they can be submitted for Binding Arbitration (Step 3). This is not inconsistent with a satisfactory resolution of interpersonal issues.

STEP 3: Binding Arbitration for Tangible Issues

Only disagreements regarding tangible issues (e.g. how a disputed expense will be paid for) are subject to arbitration.

In Binding Arbitration both parties agree before starting this formal process that they will abide by the decision of the arbitrators. Decisions made by an arbitrator are binding and are not appealable to any other body.

When arbitration is sought, the Organization will appoint a team to arbitrate. It would be inappropriate for the Director to serve as an arbitrator in this type of formal arbitration. Any documentation of the conflict will be made available to the arbitration team.

Outcome

> **Decision by arbitrator:** This is the final step in resolution of disagreements regarding tangible issues.

Summary

It is the desire of (Organization) that members and employees take definitive steps to deal with the disagreements, misunderstandings, and little irritations before they get to maturity. These are the little foxes that destroy the vines. In addition to taking care of the negative things that have great potential to hinder the work, members and employees are encouraged to give attention to the positive things that will allow God to bless the work and the workers:

For this very reason, make every effort to add to your faith goodness; and to goodness, knowledge; and to knowledge, self-control; and to self-control, perseverance; and to perseverance, godliness; and to godliness, brotherly kindness; and to brotherly kindness, love. For if you possess these qualities in increasing measure, they will keep you from being ineffective and unproductive in your knowledge of our Lord Jesus Christ. (2 Pet. 1:5-8 NIV)

This policy is used by permission from "SIL-PNG's" Employee Handbook.

Appendix C: Sample Conciliation Clauses and Helpful Facts

NOTE: The following samples are provided for information purposes only, and do not constitute legal advice. You should consult your attorney regarding the use of these provisions and the application of any specific State or Federal law to their use and enforceability.

Sample Conciliation Clauses

NOTE: Clauses A and B are generally for use in contracts with vendors, suppliers, or independent contractors.

Conciliation Clause Option A

The parties to this agreement are Christians and believe that the Bible commands them to make every effort to live at peace and to resolve disputes with each other in private or within the Christian church (see Matthew 18:15-20; 1 Corinthians 6:1-8). Therefore, the parties agree that any claim or dispute arising from or related to this agreement shall be settled by biblically-based mediation and, if necessary, legally binding arbitration in accordance with the Rules of Procedure for Christian Conciliation of the Institute for Christian Conciliation, a division of Peacemaker® Ministries (complete text of the Rules is available at www.iccpeace.com/Rules). Judgment upon an arbitration decision may be entered in any court otherwise having jurisdiction. The parties understand that these methods shall be the sole remedy for any controversy or claim arising out of this agreement and expressly waive their right to file a lawsuit in any civil court against one another for such disputes, except to enforce an arbitration decision.

Conciliation Clause Option B

Any claim or dispute arising from or related to this agreement shall be settled by mediation and, if necessary, legally binding arbitration in accordance with the Rules of Procedure for Christian Conciliation of the Institute for Christian Conciliation, a division of Peacemaker® Ministries (complete text of the Rules is available at www.iccpeace.com/Rules). Judgment upon an arbitration decision may be entered in any court otherwise having jurisdiction. The parties understand that these methods shall be the sole remedy for any controversy or claim arising out of this agreement and expressly waive their right to file a lawsuit in any civil court against one another for such disputes, except to enforce an arbitration decision.

NOTE: Clause C is useful for employment contracts, and is shown here as recommended by ASCI for Christian schools.

Conciliation Clause Option C

The parties to this agreement are Christians and believe that the Bible commands them to make every effort to live at peace and to resolve disputes with each other in private or within the Christian community in conformity with the biblical injunctions of 1 Corinthians 6:1-8, Matthew 5:23-24, and Matthew 18:15-20. Therefore, the parties agree that any claim or dispute arising out of or related to this agreement or to any aspect of the employment relationship, including claims under federal, state, and local statutory or common law, the law of contract, and law of tort, shall be settled by biblically based mediation. If the resolution of the dispute and reconciliation do not result from mediation, the matter shall then be submitted to an independent and objective arbitrator for binding arbitration.

The parties agree for the arbitration process to be conducted in accordance with the Christian Conciliation Rules of Procedure contained in the Peacemaker Ministries booklet *Guidelines for Christian Conciliation*. Consistent with these rules, each party to the agreement shall agree to the selection of the arbitrator. The parties agree that if there is an impasse in the selection of the arbitrator, the Institute for Christian Conciliation (hereafter ICC), a division of Peacemaker Ministries of Billings, Montana (800-711-7118), shall be asked to provide the name of a qualified person who will serve in that capacity. Consistent with the rules of procedure, the arbitrator shall issue a written opinion within a reasonable time.

The parties acknowledge that the resolving of conflicts requires time and financial resources. In an effort to fully encourage and implement a biblically faithful process, _____ (name of school or organization) agrees to pay all fees and expenses, which may be required by the mediator, case administrator, and/or arbitrator, related to such proceeding. The issue of final responsibility for such costs will be an agreed issue for consideration or determination in the mediation or arbitration. The parties agree they will endeavor to exchange information with each other and present the same at any mediation, or, if to arbitration pursuant to the ICC Rules of Procedure, with the intent to minimize costs and delays to the parties. They will seek to cooperate with each other and may request the mediator, case administrator, and/or arbitrator to direct and guide the preparation process so as to reasonably limit the amount of fact-finding, investigation, and discovery by the parties to that which is reasonably necessary for the parties to understand each other's issues and positions, and to prepare the matter for submission to the mediator and/or arbitrator to inform the mediator and/or arbitrator. In addition, the parties agree that in the event of an arbitration, they will use a single arbitrator who is experienced in the relevant area of law and familiar with biblical principles of resolving conflict.

The parties to this contract agree that these methods shall be the sole remedy for any controversy or claim arising out of the employment relationship or this agreement and expressly waive their right to file a lawsuit against each other in any civil court for such disputes, including any class action proceeding, except to enforce a legally binding arbitration decision. The parties acknowledge that by waiving their legal rights to file a lawsuit to resolve any dispute between them, they are not waiving their right to employ legal counsel at their own expense to assist them in any phase of the process.

Helpful Facts on Conciliation Clauses

Conciliation clauses have been used successfully for many years. The language suggested above is similar to language that has been used for decades by the American Arbitration Association.

Conciliation clauses may be used in almost any kind of contract. They are useful in employment, sales, construction, and professional services contracts.

Conciliation clauses are simple to use. Even though there are basic steps that must be followed when using them, these clauses are not complex. Once you understand the underlying concept, you may use them in many kinds of contracts.

Conciliation clauses can save you a great deal of time, money, and energy. A lawsuit can consume thousands of dollars, deplete you emotionally and spiritually, distract you from important activities and people, damage your reputation, and continue for years. A conciliation clause can help you to stay out of court and avoid many of these hardships.

Conciliation clauses can help to preserve valuable relationships. When conflict erupts over a contract and people go to court, the adversarial process often damages their relationships beyond repair. In contrast, conciliation provides a way to settle substantive issues while at the same time resolving personal differences and promoting genuine reconciliation, allowing people to resume their personal and business relationships.

Conciliation clauses are legally enforceable. Both state and federal courts will usually enforce conciliation agreements that require arbitration. If a dispute arises and either party refuses to participate in conciliation efforts, the other party may petition a court for an order to compel the parties to proceed with mediation and arbitration. Similarly, if either party files a lawsuit regarding a contract violation, the other party may ask the court to stop the suit and direct the parties to proceed with conciliation. For an example of a federal court decision upholding a clause that required Christian conciliation according to the ICC Rules of Procedure, see *Encore Productions, Inc. vs. Promise Keepers*, 53 F. Supp. 2d 1102 (D. Colorado, 1999).

Conciliation clauses do not affect other rights. When you sign a contract containing a conciliation clause, only your rights and responsibilities related to that particular agreement are affected.

The best time to agree on how to settle a conflict is before it arises. When people are initially negotiating a contract, they are usually on friendly terms and seldom expect serious problems in their relationship. If a conflict arises later, however, trust evaporates quickly; people often become defensive, suspicious, and hostile, and may refuse to agree to conciliation. Therefore, the best time to suggest using conciliation is when a contract is first being written and both sides are inclined to see a conciliation clause as a prudent, non-threatening precaution.

Conciliation clauses may be implemented even if there is not an established Christian conciliation ministry in the parties' community. The language proposed by the ICC commits the parties to a defined process, not to a particular conciliator. If a conflict develops and conciliation is necessary, the parties may ask leaders from their respective churches or other respected individuals in their community to settle the matter using the ICC Rules of Procedure. If such assistance is not easily available, they may bring in experienced conciliators from another location. (If the parties cannot agree on who will handle their case, the Rules provide that the ICC will make that decision.)

It is wise to talk with an attorney before using a conciliation clause. In some states conciliation clauses must be written in a certain way to be legally binding. For example, Montana requires that notice of arbitration provisions be printed on the front page of a contract in underlined capital letters (e.g., "THIS CONTRACT IS SUBJECT TO ARBITRATION UNDER THE MONTANA ARBITRATION ACT, TITLE 27, CHAPTER 5, MONTANA CODE ANNOTATED"). Texas requires that certain arbitration clauses be signed by legal counsel, and California has special requirements for clauses involving medical malpractice or real estate transactions. A visit with an attorney can confirm your commitment to avoid litigation, alert you to local requirements, and ensure the enforceability of a conciliation clause in your contract.

The ICC has materials that can help you explain the benefits of using conciliation clauses. One of the best ways to persuade other people to agree to use a conciliation clause is to encourage them to visit our web site and provide them with copies of a Peacemaking Principles pamphlet and these guidelines.

If you begin using conciliation clauses today, you are taking a wise precaution against unnecessary stress and expense in the future. Moreover, by openly committing yourself to the conflict resolution principles set forth in Scripture, you will be making a clear statement that you trust in God and desire to follow his principles in every aspect of your life.

For more information on the use of conciliation clauses, please visit www.iccpeace.com, Conciliation Clauses.

Endnotes

1. *Six Tips to Managing Workplace Conflict*, Rachel Zupek, and CareerBuilder 2009.
2. *Six Tips to Managing Workplace Conflict*, Rachel Zupek, and CareerBuilder 2009.
3. http://www.vitalsmarts.com/userfiles/File/Research/Time Wasted Conflict.pdf.
4. *The Cost of Conflict in the Workplace*, by James A. Cram and Richard K. MacWilliams, Cramby River Consultants.
5. CPP, Inc – a research firm.
6. *Managing Differences: How to Build Better Relationships at Work and Home*, (2005, 4th ed.) Dana, Daniel *Insights into Employee Motivation, Commitment and Retention*, 2002, Kreisman, Barbara.
7. *Personnel Journal*.
8. Global Business and Economic Round Table on Addictions and Mental Health.
9. *HR Magazine*.
10. *HR Magazine*.
11. An excellent book focused on integrating your faith in your work is *Mastering Monday*, John D. Beckett, Intervarsity Press, 2006.
12. American Center for Law & Justice: Religious Activities by Employers under Title VII, http://www.acji.org/issues/Resources/Document.aspx?ID=872; Kolodziej v. Smith, 588 N.E.2d 634 (Mass. 1992).
13. American Center for Law & Justice: Religious Activities by Employers under Title VII, http://www.acji.org/issues/Resources/Document.aspx?ID=872.
14. This information is provided for general information and not as legal advice.
15. See www.iccpeace.com/Rules to see the Rules of Procedure for Christian Conciliation. You can also find Frequently Asked Questions about Christian Conciliation online at www.iccpeace.com/FAQs under "Frequently Asked Questions."
16. This conciliation clause is taken from the employment contract clause developed for ASCI schools. See Appendix C for additional clause samples and the complete language that may be considered.